A Bear's Tale

Relato de un oso

THIS EDITION

Editorial Management by Oriel Square
Produced for DK by WonderLab Group LLC
Jennifer Emmett, Erica Green, Kate Hale, *Founders*

Editor Maya Myers; **Photography Editor** Nicole DiMella; **Managing Editor** Rachel Houghton;
Designers Project Design Company; **Researcher** Michelle Harris;
Copy Editor Lori Merritt; **Indexer** Connie Binder; **Proofreader** Carmen Orozco;
Authenticity Reader Dr. Naomi R. Caldwell; **Spanish Translation** Isabel C. Mendoza;
Series Reading Specialist Dr. Jennifer Albro

First American Edition, 2024
Published in the United States by DK Publishing, a division of Penguin Random House LLC
1745 Broadway, 20th Floor, New York, NY 10019

A catalog record for this book is available from the Library of Congress.
HC ISBN: 978-0-7440-9491-6
PB ISBN: 978-0-7440-9490-9

DK books are available at special discounts when purchased in bulk for sales promotions, premiums, fund-raising,
or educational use. For details, contact:
DK Publishing Special Markets, 1745 Broadway, 20th Floor, New York, NY 10019
SpecialSales@dk.com

Printed and bound in China

The publisher would like to thank the following for their kind permission to reproduce their images:
a=above; c=center; b=below; l=left; r=right; t=top; b/g=background

Alamy Stock Photo: All Canada Photos / Bob Gurr 16-17, All Canada Photos / Dave Blackey 8-9, All Canada Photos /
Stephen J. Krasemann 17bc, Design Pics Inc / Alaska Stock RF / Doug Lindstrand 7br, 20bc, Design Pics Inc / Wave
Royalty Free, Inc. 13br, 23clb, FLPA 20crb, Rolf Hicker Photography 3, Jason O. Watson (USA: Alaska photographs) 8bc,
Westend61 GmbH / Fotofeeling 16bc, 23cla **Bridgeman Images:** Gift Of Elizabeth H. Penn 9bl; **Dreamstime.com:**
David Burke 19br, Antonio Guillem 12-13, 14-15, Klomsky 1, Derrick Neill 7bc, Ovydyborets 19bl, Joe Sohm 9br, Wirestock
11b, Maria Zebroff 18bc; **Getty Images:** Moment / Colleen Gara 4-5, 23cl, Moment / Jared Lloyd 6-7, Photodisc / Don
Grall 10-11, 23bl, Stone / Paul Souders 14bc, 15bl, 15bc, The Image Bank / Mark Newman 13bl, 20-21, Universal Images
Group / Education Images 18-19; **Getty Images / iStock:** Jillian Cooper 22, 23tl, DigitalVision Vectors / mecaleha 4bl,
6bc, llvllagic 10bc; **Shutterstock.com:** EVGENNI 21b, saraporn 17br; **VectorStock:** renreeser 12bc

Cover images: *Front:* **Dreamstime.com:** Anastasiya Aheyeva;
Back: **Dreamstime.com:** Pavel Naumov cb; **Getty Images / iStock:** PCH-Vector cra

All other images © Dorling Kindersley
For more information see: www.dkimages.com

www.dk.com

A Bear's Tale
Relato de un oso

Alli Brydon

Summer begins.
A grizzly bear walks
on four feet.
The bear walks in its home.
Its home is the woods.

Comienza el verano.
Un oso pardo camina en
sus cuatro patas.
El oso camina en su hogar.
Su hogar es el bosque.

grizzly bear
oso pardo

The bear is big.
The bear is strong.

El oso es grande.
El oso es fuerte.

claws

garras

It can stay alive
in the wild.

Es capaz de sobrevivir en
estado salvaje.

fur
pelaje

People honor the bear. They think bears are brave and smart. People make art about bears. They tell stories about them.

Hay personas que veneran al oso. Creen que los osos son valientes e inteligentes. Hacen obras de arte sobre los osos. Cuentan historias sobre ellos.

art

arte

People stay away from the bear.
This is also a way they honor it.
The grizzly walks in the woods alone.

woods

bosque

La gente se mantiene
alejada del oso.
Es otra manera
de venerarlo.
El oso pardo camina
solo por el bosque.

mountain
montaña

marks

marcas

The bear marks a tree. The marks tell other bears to stay away.

El oso marca un árbol. Las marcas les indican a otros osos que deben alejarse.

fight

pelea

But if another bear
comes, the bears fight.
The bear is hurt,
but it stays strong.

Pero si otro oso se acerca,
los osos pelean.
El oso sale
lastimado, pero se
mantiene fuerte.

The air turns cool in fall.
Soon, it will be winter.
The bear digs a den.

En el otoño, el aire se enfría.
Pronto llegará el invierno.
El oso excava para hacerse
un cubil.

den

cubil

It will rest here
for the winter.
First, the bear must
fill its belly.

Aquí descansará
durante el invierno.
Primero, tiene que
llenarse la panza.

The bear hunts for
fish to eat.
People also hunt fish.
The bear picks berries.
People also eat berries.

El oso caza peces
para comérselos.
La gente también
caza peces.
El oso come bayas.
La gente también
come bayas.

fish

pez

It is winter.
The woods are cold.
There is little food to eat.
It is time for the bear to
rest. It goes in its den.

Llega el invierno.
Hace frío en el bosque.
Hay poco para comer.
Es hora de que el oso
descanse. Se mete
a su cubil.

rest

descansar

Spring comes. The bear has cubs! Now, there are more bears. The bears walk in the forest. Soon, it will be summer again.

Llega la primavera. ¡La osa tiene oseznos! Ahora hay más osos. Los osos caminan por el bosque. Pronto regresará el verano.

Glossary
Glosario

cubs
baby bears

den
a cave or place bears dig for shelter

grizzly bear
a large kind of bear

marks
indentations left by something

woods
forest

bosque
lugar lleno de árboles

cubil
una caverna o un lugar que el oso cava para refugiarse

marcas
hendiduras que se hacen sobre alguna cosa

oseznos
las crías del oso

oso pardo
un tipo de oso que es grande

Quiz
Prueba

Answer the questions to see what you have learned. Check your answers with an adult.

1. Where do grizzly bears live?

2. How do people honor bears?

3. How can a bear tell other animals to stay away?

4. What are some foods that bears eat?

5. Where does a bear rest during the winter?

1. Woods 2. Through art and stories 3. By marking trees
4. Fish and berries 5. In a den

Responde las preguntas para saber cuánto aprendiste. Verifica tus respuestas con un adulto.

1. ¿Dónde viven los osos pardos?

2. ¿Qué hace la gente para venerar a los osos?

3. ¿Qué hace un oso para decirles a otros animales que deben alejarse?

4. ¿Cuáles son algunas de las cosas que comen los osos?

5. ¿Dónde descansa un oso durante el invierno?

1. En el bosque 2. Hacen obras de arte y cuentan historias
3. Hacen marcas en los árboles 4. Peces y bayas 5. En un cubil